# Language Sprout™

# FRANÇAIS
## 1

### cahier d'activités
French Activity Book

Copyright © 2017 Language Sprout Publishing, L.L.C.
ISBN: 978-1-63354-037-8
All rights reserved. Published in the United States by Language Sprout.

languagesprout.com

# Workbook Level Summary

## Level 0

All about the the French alphabet and French basics. Go on an adventure with the Sprout friends made for emerging learners.

YOU ARE HERE

## Level 1

Meet the Sprout Friends and build a vocabulary foundation! Learn to count and call out shapes and colors. Share stories about pets and even help Rebe make her super noodle soup. Grammar: To Have and To Want

## Level 2

Marisol arrives! Figure out which fruits this little dinosaur will and will not eat. Dream about jobs along with the Sprout Friends and get ready to take off with transportation. Allons-y! Grammar: To Like, To Be, To Go

## Level 3

Build a monster using body part vocab. Describe feelings, weather and where you are from. Then form a huge robot family while learning to name each member! Grammar: To Be, To Do/Make, The Date

## Level 4

Make a mask and find a cape. Join in the super hero action inside and outside the classroom. Name that classroom item and bring verbs to life...with the Sprout Friends, of course! Grammar: Verb + Infinitives, To be able

# Workbook Level Summary

## Level 5

Add to the drama in Project Grant then find out if your favorite foods will ever be enough to satisfy Leroy. Finally, grab a map because we have to find Shazam! Grammar: Regular ER, RE and IR verbs

## Level 6

Alarm clocks ring and clocks chime. Start the day with Bob and get ready to race against the clock. Take a shopping trip with Lulu but don't get home late. Grammar: Irregular verbs, Time, Reflexive Verbs

## Level 7

Pepe hasn't always lived in Sprout City. Look back and get ready to tell stories about "when you were little." Grammar: Passé composé, Imperfect, Frequency, Command Verbs.

## Level 8

Search, discover and navigate with Emma on a big Sproutland adventure. Tell the tallest tales as your travel, survival and geography vocabulary grows. Grammar: Conditional, Gerund, Future

Visit us at

www.LanguageSprout.com

for more information about Levels 9 - 16!

# Table of Contents

- [ ] **I: Numbers, Colors & Shapes**
  - [ ] Bienvenue! — 2
  - [ ] Les Numéros! — 3-7
  - [ ] Écris!! — 8
  - [ ] Va à la pêche! — 9
  - [ ] Les Couleurs — 10-11
  - [ ] Pratique! — 12
  - [ ] Dessine! — 13
  - [ ] Les Formes — 14
  - [ ] Pratique! — 15
  - [ ] Questions — 16
  - [ ] Colorions! — 17, 18
  - [ ] Action! — 19

- [ ] **II: House Animals & "To Have"**
  - [ ] Les Animaux domestiques — 24-27
  - [ ] Quel est ton animal préféré? — 27
  - [ ] Pratique! — 28
  - [ ] Mots-Cachés — 29
  - [ ] Dessine! — 30
  - [ ] Le Genre et le Français — 31
  - [ ] Essaie! — 32
  - [ ] Articles — 33
  - [ ] Essaie! — 34
  - [ ] Articles — 35
  - [ ] Traductions — 36
  - [ ] Pronoms — 37
  - [ ] Essaie! — 38
  - [ ] «Avoir» — 39
  - [ ] Colorions! — 40
  - [ ] Plus de traductions — 41

# Table of Contents

- ☐ Lis! — 42
- ☐ Description Visuelle — 43

☐ **III: Vegetables & "To Want"**

- ☐ Les Légumes — 48-52
- ☐ Je préfère! — 53
- ☐ Pratique! — 54
- ☐ Dessine! — 55
- ☐ Mots-Cachés — 56
- ☐ Traductions — 57
- ☐ «Vouloir» — 58
- ☐ Plus de traductions — 59
- ☐ Lis! — 60
- ☐ Description Visuelle — 61

☐ Tous ensemble — 65

# Symbols

Look for these symbols throughout your new workbook!

☐ **TEACHER'S CHECK-BOX**

🔊 **AUDIO AVAILABLE***

When you see this one, 🔊 stop and listen carefully to a recording demonstrating how to say each vocabulary word.

Your «professeur» will use this one: ☐.
Once you have learned a set of words, the boxes will be checked and you will be ready for the next set of vocabulary words!

*NOTE:

In addition to French vocabulary pronunciation, a NARRATED VERSION of workbook instructions and grammar descriptions is also available.

## Bienvenue! - Welcome!

# Way to go!

You made a great decision to learn FRENCH. We are so proud of you!

So many amazing doors and opportunities will open up to you through your studies.

Just keep up the good work, and don't forget to look for the secret fun!

## Let's get started!

"Bonjour" is how we say "Hello."

"Au revoir" is how we say "Good bye."

# Les Numéros

Practice writing the French word for each number at least four times.

un  _____  _____  _____  _____

deux  _____  _____  _____  _____

trois  _____  _____  _____  _____

quatre  _____  _____  _____  _____

cinq  _____  _____  _____  _____

six  _____  _____  _____  _____

# Les Numéros

Practice writing the French word for each number at least four times.

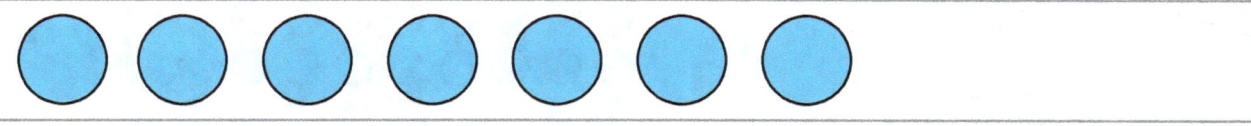

sept _____

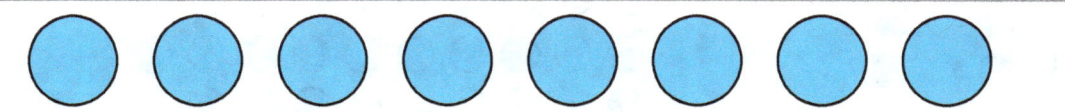

huit _____

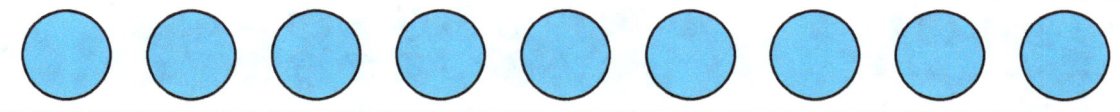

neuf _____

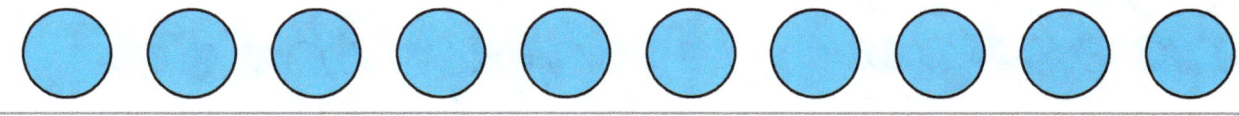

dix _____

• • • • • • • • • • • • • • • • • • • • • • • • • • • • • •

## Can we count it higher?
## Oh yeah...

11 onze _____      16 seize _____
12 douze _____     17 dix-sept _____
13 treize _____    18 dix-huit _____
14 quatorze _____  19 dix-neuf _____
15 quinze _____    20 vingt _____

# Les Numéros

## Compter par dizaines! *Counting by ten!*

dix
10

vingt
20

trente
30

quarante
40

cinquante
50

soixante
60

soixante-dix
70

quatre-vingts
80

quatre-vingt-dix
90

cent
100

# Les Numéros

## Tout ce qui se trouve entre
*Everything in between*

What about all the numbers in between? Like 27, or 53, or 99? Start with the base number and follow it with the in between number. So, 27 will be the base number 20 (vingt) followed by the in between number 7 (sept). That makes vingt-sept! Now let's take a closer look.

### 21, 31, 41, 51, 61...

In order to say 21, we are going to squeeze the French word **et** (and) in between VINGT and UN, to say vingt-et-un. We do the same for 31 (trente-et-un), 41 (quarante-et-un), 51 (cinquante-et-un), and 61 (soixante-et-un).

- 20 vingt
- 21 vingt-et-un
- 22 vingt-deux
- 23 vingt-trois
- 24 vingt-quatre
- 25 vingt-cinq
- 26 vingt-six
- 27 vingt-sept
- 28 vingt-huit
- 29 vingt-neuf

### 70'S, 80'S, 90'S

In French, to say 70, we simply say the word for 60 (soixante) followed by the word for 10 (dix) to get soixante-dix. To say 80, we say the word for four followed by the word for 20: quatre-vingt (four-twenty). Then, to say 90, we just add a 10 to that: quatre-vingt-dix. So 99 would be quatre-vingt-dix-neuf.

- 71 soixante-onze
- 76 soixante-seize
- 81 quatre-vingt-un
- 90 quatre-vingt-dix
- 95 quatre-vingt-quinze
- 73 soixante-treize
- 79 soixante-dix-neuf
- 88 quatre-vingt-huit
- 92 quatre-vingt-douze
- 99 quatre-vingt-dix-neuf

# Écris!

Write each of the numbers in the boxes below.

| | | |
|---|---|---|
| trois | onze | sept |
| vingt-deux | quatre-vingt-treize | treize |
| quatre | soixante-seize | quarante-cinq |
| cinquante-trois | trente-neuf | quatre-vingt-quatre |

# Va à la pêche!

"Va à la pêche!" is how we say "Go Fish!" in French.

Here are the phrases we need to play:

|  |  |
|---|---|
| Do you have a _____ ? | Est-ce que tu as un _____ ? |
| Yes, I have one. | Oui, j'en ai un! |
| No, I don't have it. Go fish! | Non, je n'en ai pas, va à la pêche! |
| Thank you. | Merci. |

# Les Couleurs

Practice writing the French word for each color at least four times.

red
☐ rouge     rouge  _____  _____  _____  _____

orange
☐ orange    _____  _____  _____  _____

yellow
☐ jaune     _____  _____  _____  _____

green
☐ vert      _____  _____  _____  _____

blue
☐ bleu      _____  _____  _____  _____

purple
☐ violet    _____  _____  _____  _____

# Les Couleurs

Practice writing the French word for each color at least four times.

pink ☐ rose _____ _____ _____ _____

sky blue ☐ bleu ciel _____ _____ _____ _____

brown ☐ marron _____ _____ _____ _____

black ☐ noir _____ _____ _____ _____

white ☐ blanc _____ _____ _____ _____

grey ☐ gris _____ _____ _____ _____

11

## Pratique!
# VOCABULARY PRACTICE!

Match each color to both its English and French word.

|  | |  |
|---|---|---|
| green | 🟧 orange bar | violet |
| purple | 🟧 orange bar | bleu |
| blue | 🟨 yellow bar | rouge |
| orange | 🟩 green bar | jaune |
| red | 🟪 purple bar | orange |
| yellow | 🟪 lavender bar | vert |

|  | |  |
|---|---|---|
| black | 🟪 pink bar | blanc |
| sky blue | 🟦 light blue bar | gris |
| white | 🟫 brown bar | noir |
| grey | ⬛ black bar | bleu ciel |
| pink | ⬜ white bar | marron |
| brown | ⬜ grey bar | rose |

# Dessine!

Draw something in each of the colors in the boxes below.

| | | |
|---|---|---|
| jaune | bleu ciel | noir |
| orange | violet | gris |
| bleu | rouge | rose |
| blanc | marron | vert |

# Les Formes

le cercle
☐ circle

le carré
☐ square

le rectangle
☐ rectangle

l'ovale
☐ oval

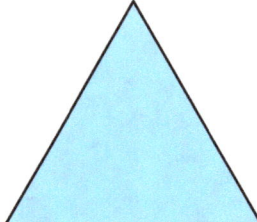

le triangle
☐ triangle

le losange
☐ diamond

le pentagone
☐ pentagon

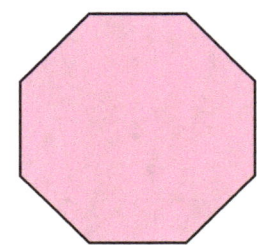

l'octagone
☐ octagon

le coeur
☐ heart

l'étoile
☐ star

le croissant
☐ crescent

l'hexagone
☐ hexagon

## Pratique!

# VOCABULARY PRACTICE!

Match each shape to both its English and French word.

## Questions

**De quelle couleur est..?**  What color is...?

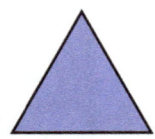 1. De quelle couleur est le triangle?
Le triangle est...
_____

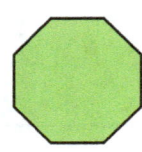 2. De quelle couleur est l'octogone?
_____

 3. De quelle couleur est l'étoile?
_____

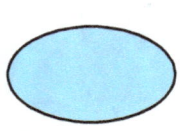 4. De quelle couleur est l'ovale?
_____

 5. De quelle couleur est le carré?
_____

**Quelle forme est..?**  Which shape is...?

1. Quelle forme est le rose?
_____

2. Quelle forme est le jaune?
_____

3. Quelle forme est le violet?
_____

4. Quelle forme est le vert?
_____

5. Quelle forme est le bleu?
_____

# Colorions!

| 1. rouge | 4. vert | 7. rose |
| 2. orange | 5. bleu | 8. noir |
| 3. jaune | 6. violet | 9. marron |

Remember: Areas without numbers can remain <<blanc>>

# Colorions!

| 1. rouge | 4. vert | 7. rose |
| 2. orange | 5. bleu | 8. noir |
| 3. jaune | 6. violet | 9. marron |

Remember: Areas without numbers can remain <<blanc>>

# Action!

Let's put it all together!
Read the phrases below and draw what it says in each box.

| | | |
|---|---|---|
| cinq coeurs noirs | quatre carrés verts | neuf étoiles jaunes |
| un triangle gris | deux hexagones verts | deux ovales oranges |
| trois pentagones blancs | sept croissants marron | six cercles rouges |
| un rectangle bleu ciel | douze carrés roses | huit losanges bleus |

# La Révision

## Les nombres:

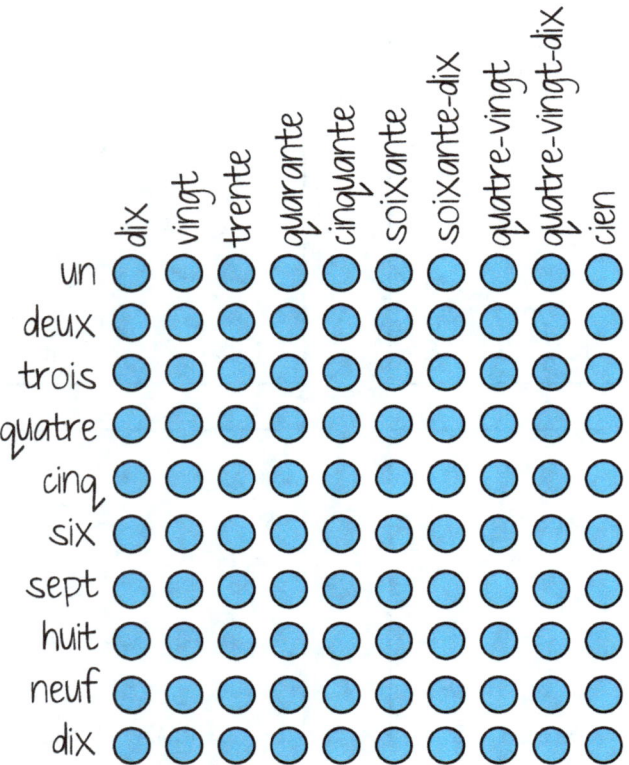

## Les formes:

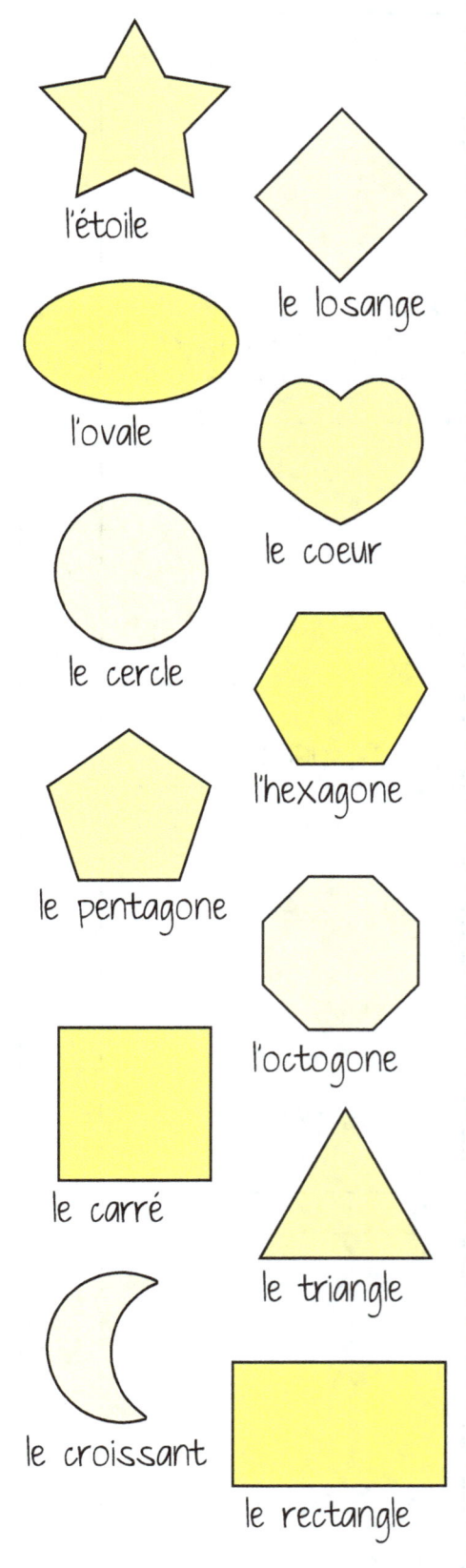

- l'étoile
- le losange
- l'ovale
- le coeur
- le cercle
- l'hexagone
- le pentagone
- l'octogone
- le carré
- le triangle
- le croissant
- le rectangle

## Les couleurs:

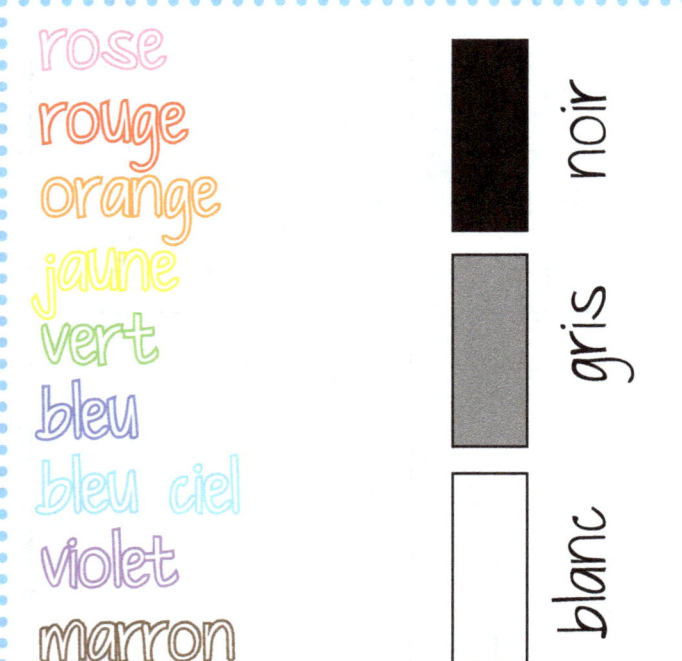

rose
rouge
orange
jaune
vert
bleu
bleu ciel
violet
marron

noir
gris
blanc

# Test - Niveau 1 ★ 1  _____

Nom

Use the following row of shapes to answer questions 1 - 4.
En français, s'il vous plaît!

● ● ● ● ● ● ● ● ● ●

1) Combien de cercles sont bleues? _____

2) Combien de cercles sont oranges? _____

3) Combien de cercles sont roses? _____

4) Combien de cercles sont verts? _____

Circle the correct word to match each sentence to its picture

5) C'est une étoile / croissant jaune. ★

6) C'est un ovale rouge / violet. ⬭

7) C'est un hexagone / octogone bleu ciel. ⬢

8) C'est un coeur blanc / gris. ♡

Draw a picture to match each phrase below.

| 9) | 10) | 11) |
|---|---|---|
| sept rectangles marron | dix croissants rouges | cinq pentagones noirs |

# Test - Niveau 1 ★ 1

_____
Nom

How many circles are in each group?
Write your answer in the space provided.
En français, s'il vous plaît!

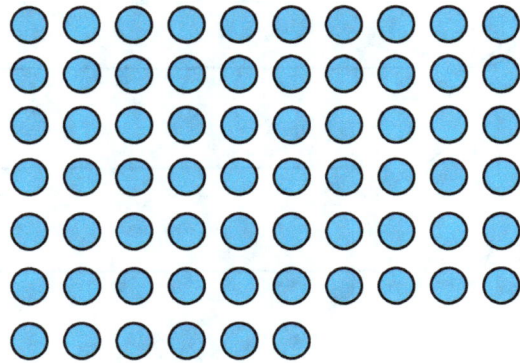

12) _____

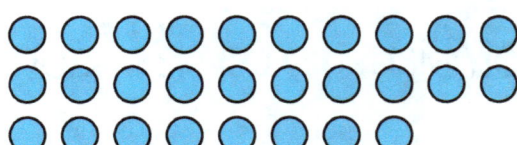

13) _____

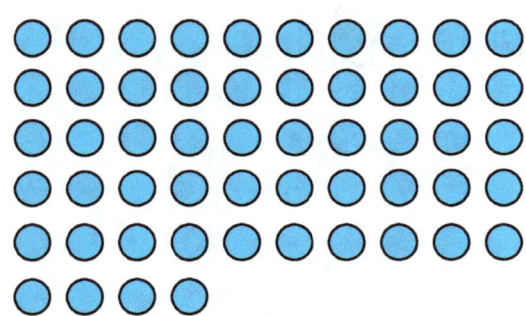

14) _____

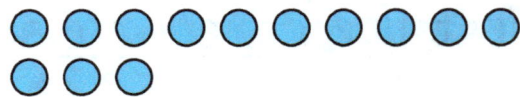

15) _____

Bon travail!

That means "Good job!"

**TEACHER'S CORNER**

Progress Score:

Numbers_____
Colors_____
Shapes_____

QUIZ_____

Ready for Level 1-2 ? ☐

# Unité II
# Les Animaux domestiques et «Avoir»

# Les Animaux domestiques

Practice writing the French word for each animal at least four times.

**le chien**
☐ dog

**le hamster**
☐ hamster

**la tortue**
☐ turtle

**le lapin**
☐ rabbit

# Les Animaux domestiques

**le poisson**
☐ fish

**le lézard**
☐ lizard

**la grenouille**
☐ frog

**le dinosaure**
☐ dinosaur

# Les Animaux domestiques

le chat
☐ cat

l'oiseau
☐ bird

le furet
☐ ferret

le papillon
☐ butterfly

# Les Animaux domestiques

le cobaye
☐ guinea pig

l'escargot
☐ snail

## Quel est ton animal préféré?

Draw your favorite of the animals you just learned in the box.

Mon animal préféré est _____
et il est de couleur _____

## Pratique!
# VOCABULARY PRACTICE!

In the corresponding space, write the French word for each animal.

1) le cobaye
2) _____
3) _____
4) _____
5) _____
6) _____
7) _____

1) _____
2) _____
3) _____
4) _____
5) _____
6) _____
7) _____

# Mots-Cachés

```
L A P I N O T R E Z O G B L D
K U L V C G R E N O U I L L E
F Z I L O N V B C H I E N Q I
U E T K C O L T R Z K S E T Y
R K O P H A H G F R I Y K N M
E I R B O D I N O S A U R E O
T S T I N L N P P Q Z A N L X
U P U W D O I S E A U A D C H
Y L E N I M W J N B O U I H A
C U A I N G P O I S S O N A M
O L P N D W Q I O A B L N T S
B L J H E E S C A R G O T E T
A W M I O L N Q S S R Z N R E
Y L E Z A R D I J A E Q Z A R
E L W U A P A P I L L O N Z T
```

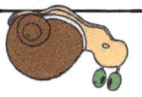

## Banque de mots

Find the following words in French in the puzzle above.

| | | |
|---|---|---|
| FERRET | BUTTERFLY | SNAIL |
| FROG | HAMSTER | DINOSAUR |
| FISH | GUINEA PIG | LIZARD |
| DOG | TURTLE | BIRD |
| CAT | | RABBIT |

29

# Dessine!

Draw what is described in each of the boxes below.

| | | |
|---|---|---|
| 3 escargots noirs | 5 chats blancs | 7 cobayes violets |
| 2 chiens marron | 4 furets gris | 9 poissons jaunes |
| 10 tortues verts | 3 papillons rouges | Un hamster bleu |
| 5 dinosaures bleu ciel | 4 oiseaux bleus | Une grenouille rouge |

# Le Genre et le Français

**Gender and the French Language...** what on earth could the two have to do with one another? We wondered that at first too! But French and <u>lots</u> of other languages use gender.

What this means is that EVERYTHING in French has been assigned either a **masculine** (boy) or **feminine** (girl) identity.

**BASIC RULE**: In French, sometimes the ending of a word tells us its gender.
Words ending with **consonants** are **masculine** (boy).
Words ending with the vowel **e** are **feminine** (girl).

At times this makes sense and gives us information about the actual gender of something. <u>For example</u>:

garçon = boy                    infirmier = male nurse
fille = girl        and         infirmière = female nurse

But as soon as we start talking about something other than a person or an animal, the gender assignment simply makes no sense. <u>Check it out</u>:

chemisier = a girl's shirt (masculine)
cravate = a man's necktie (feminine)

So, start paying attention to word endings
and remember the **BASIC RULE**!

But wait just a second. Have you noticed that plenty of words don't follow these rules? French is full of **REBELS** who don't follow the **BASIC RULES**. But hey, even **REBELS** have rules. You're going to need to know some **REBEL RULES** to keep things organized

## Masculine Words
★ Often end in **consonants** (d,n,t,r...)
★ Often end in a vowel that is NOT **e**
★ Often end in **eur**
★ Sometimes end in **e**
(like most shapes)

## Feminine Words
★ Often end in **e**
★ Often end in **ion**
★ Often end in **lle** or **tte**
★ Often end in **tie** or **té**
★ Often end in **euse**

# Essaie!

Let's try it out!

Place an **M** next to masculine words and an **F** next to feminine words.

| | | | |
|---|---|---|---|
| _____ | oiseau | _____ | grenouille |
| _____ | fille | _____ | chaise |
| _____ | chat | _____ | triangle |
| _____ | poisson | _____ | école |
| _____ | tortue | _____ | carré |
| _____ | lapin | _____ | bain |
| _____ | dinosaure | _____ | losange |
| _____ | papillon | _____ | lavabo |
| _____ | chien | _____ | étoile |
| _____ | ours | _____ | université |
| _____ | grand-mère | _____ | table |
| _____ | amie | _____ | citrouille |
| _____ | rectangle | _____ | maïs |
| _____ | ananas | _____ | chaussure |
| _____ | banane | _____ | chapeau |
| _____ | croissant | _____ | porte |

# Articles

So...why do I care about all this gender stuff anyway?

Okay, that is a totally valid question. What does figuring out the gender have to do with the price of tuna fish in France?

In French, articles (and adjectives) **Shape Shift** to match their noun!

Here's the deal: The gender assignment of a noun is going to change its article. In English all words can use the article "the" but in French there are three different ways of saying "the!" Overkill, we know, so let's all appreciate English for a minute...

## The word "the"

In French, **the** changes based on the gender of the word:

Le = the (masculine)
La = the (feminine)

Now hold the phone. That's only two.
Well, if there's only one of something, then we use le or la, but...
If the word is plural (meaning more than one):

LES = the (masculine or feminine)

### Let's recap it:

| How many? | Masculine | Feminine |
|---|---|---|
| 1 | ☐ le | ☐ la |
| 2+ | ☐ les | ☐ les |

Also, the gender assisgnment of a noun changes any adjectives attached to it. Depending on the gender (and number), in order to describe something green, you might say vert, verte, verts, or vertes.

# Essaie!

## Let's try it out!

Write "the" in French by placing le, la, l', or les next to each word.

| | | | |
|---|---|---|---|
| _____ | oiseau | _____ | grenouille |
| _____ | fille | _____ | chaises |
| _____ | chat | _____ | triangles |
| _____ | cobaye | _____ | école |
| _____ | tortues | _____ | carré |
| _____ | lapin | _____ | bains |
| _____ | dinosaure | _____ | jeu |
| _____ | papillon | _____ | lavabo |
| _____ | chien | _____ | étoiles |
| _____ | furets | _____ | université |
| _____ | grand-mères | _____ | table |
| _____ | amie | _____ | citrouilles |
| _____ | oncle | _____ | maïs |
| _____ | hexagone | _____ | chaussure |
| _____ | bananes | _____ | chapeau |
| _____ | croissant | _____ | portes |

★Drop the vowel in the article Le or La and change it to just L' when the following noun also starts with a vowel.

# Articles

Okay, so we already know that there are three different ways to say "the." But there are also three ways to say "a," "an," and "some."

So just like with "the," **the word "a"** changes based on the gender of the word.
So, if you wanted to say "I have a fish," or "I have an apple"...

**un** = a or an (masculine)
**une** = a or an (feminine)

But that's just two ways.
Well, if there is only one of something, then we use un or une, but...
If the word is plural (meaning more than one):

**des** = some (masculine)
**des** = some (feminine)

## Let's recap it:

| How many? | Masculine | Feminine |
|---|---|---|
| 1 | ☐ un | ☐ une |
| 2+ | ☐ des | ☐ des |

## Let's try it out!
Write "a," "an," or "some" in French by placing un, une, or des next to each word.

_____ oiseau          _____ grenouilles

_____ fille           _____ amie

_____ chat            _____ amis

_____ cobaye          _____ carrés

_____ tortue          _____ bananes

_____ lapin           _____ carotte

# Traductions

Translate each phrase from French to English, or English to French.
(Remember that in French, adjectives usually come <u>after</u> the noun.)

1) Des tortues roses.
_____

2) L'oiseau jaune.
_____

3) Le papillon bleu.
_____

4) Les chats noirs.
_____

5) Les grenouilles vertes.
_____

6) The brown guinea pig.
_____

7) The orange hamsters.
_____

8) Some black dogs.
_____

9) The green dinosaur.
_____

10) The sky blue ferret.
_____

*Qu'est-ce qui se cache sur cette page? What is hiding on this page?*

# Pronoms

**pronouns** are amazing helper words that we have to take the place of **nouns**.

What exactly is a **noun**?

A **noun** is a person, place or thing - such as: a squirrel, a marker or Katie.

A **pronoun** helps us in a sentence so that we <u>don't</u> have to say the full name of the **noun** over and over again.

For example:

**Katie McAndrews** sits on the table. Then **Katie McAndrews** stands up.

We can replace **Katie McAndrews** with **she**.

The sentence then becomes:

**She** sits on the table. Then **she** stands up.

<mark>TAH DAH!</mark> Much easier. (sounds better too, right?)

## Les pronoms en français:

| | | | |
|---|---|---|---|
| ☐ | je<br>I | ☐ | nous<br>we |
| ☐ | tu<br>you | ☐ | vous<br>you (plural) |
| ☐ | il<br>he | ☐ | ils<br>they (masculine) |
| ☐ | elle<br>she | ☐ | elles<br>they (feminine) |

# Essaie!

Match each English pronoun with its French equivalent.

she — elles
I — nous
they (masculine) — je
he — elle
we — il
you — tu
you (plural) — vous
they (feminine) — ils

Wrtie the pronoun (en Français, por favor) that replaces the noun(s).

1) Lulú
   elle

2) Pépé
   _____

3) Lily et Marta
   _____

4) Bob et Pépé
   _____

5) Trois papillons et moi
   _____

6) Marisol, Marta et Bob
   _____

7) Pépé et un chien
   _____

8) Shazam et moi
   _____

9) Lulú et moi (me)
   _____

10) Marta et le cobaye
    _____

# «Avoir»

## The verb AVOIR means to have in French.

In French, just like in English, we need to <u>conjugate</u> our verb. What that means is that we have to change it slightly so that it <u>matches</u> the person who is speaking. Then we just add the thing we have.

### Avoir

| | | | |
|---|---|---|---|
| ☐ | j'ai<br>I have | ☐ | nous avons<br>we have |
| ☐ | tu as<br>you have | ☐ | vous avez<br>you (plural) have |
| ☐ | il a<br>he has | ☐ | ils ont<br>they (masculine) have |
| ☐ | elle a<br>she has | ☐ | elles ont<br>they (feminine) have |

**Check it out:** I have a dog.
(J'ai = I have) + (un chien = a dog).
J'ai un chien.

**NO WAY!** In French, to say "don't have" you make a sandwich around the verb avoir with "ne" first, "avoir" in the middle and "pas" last.

I don't have = Je n'ai pas
You don't have = Tu n'as pas
She doesn't have = Elle n'a pas
We don't have = Nous n'avons pas
You all don't have = Vous n'avez pas
They don't have = Ils n'ont pas

**Note:** In negative sentences "un" and "une" often turn to "de" after "pas."
Example 1: Elle a un chat. Elle n'a pas de chat.
Example 2: Nous avons une tortue. Nous n'avons pas de tortue.
Pretty easy, right? Now it's practice time!

# Colorions!

Match each color with the correct form of the French verb
<<avoir>>

"I have" = vert     "We have" = violet

"You have = rose

"She has" = marron     "They have" = rouge

Remember: Areas without numbers can remain <<blanc>>

# Plus de traductions

Translate each phrase from French to English or English to French.

1) J'ai trois oiseaux bleus.
_____

2) Nous avons cinq grenouilles vertes.
_____

3) Elle n'a pas de chat gris.
_____

4) Ils ont un lézard orange.
_____

5) Vous n'avez pas de chien.
_____

6) You have a black cat.
_____

7) We have five purple butterflies.
_____

8) She doesn't have a ferret.
_____

9) They have some lizards.
_____

10) He has a dinosaur.

Qu'est-ce qui se cache sur cette page? What is hiding on this page?

# Lis!

Read the paragraph, then answer the questions below.

> Ma classe a huit enfants. Tous les enfants ont un animal de compagnie. J'ai un chien marron et noir. Mon chien s'appelle Pascal. Pépé n'a pas de chien, mais il a cinq escargots blancs. Bob a un lapin et deux oiseaux. L'un est vert, et l'autre est violet. Lulú et Rébé ont un furet. Le furet s'appelle Squinkles. Emma a un chat et un hamster gris. Son hamster s'appelle Fleur et son chat s'appelle Léon. Lily a quinze papillons mais n'a pas de dinosaure. Enfin, Marta a une tortue.

1) Combien d'enfants ont des animaux domestiques?
_____

2) Comment s'appelle le hamster d'Emma?
_____

3) De quelle couleur sont les oiseaux de Bob?
_____

4) Qu'est-ce que Lily a?
_____

5) Qu'est-ce que Lily n'a pas?
_____

# Description Visuelle

Read the paragraphs below.
Draw what it says inside the box.

Bob a un chien blanc, mais n'a pas de chat gris. Emma a un oiseau bleu et deux cochons d'Inde jaunes et marron.

Bob                    Emma

Pépé a quatre lézards. Un est vert, un autre est jaune, et deux sont violets. Son amie Lily a deux chats blancs et deux poissons rouges. Ils n'ont pas de chat gris ni de lapin rose. Sa maman a un escargot orange.

Pépé                   Lily

# La Révision

## LES ANIMAUX:

- le cobaye
- l'oiseau
- le poisson
- le dinosaure
- la grenouille
- le papillon
- la tortue
- le hamster
- l'escargot
- le furet
- le lapin
- le chien
- le lézard
- le chat

## PRONOMS ET AVOIR:

| | |
|---|---|
| j'ai<br>I have | nous avons<br>we have |
| tu as<br>you have | vous avez<br>you (plural) have |
| il a<br>he has | ils ont<br>they (masculine) have |
| elle a<br>she has | elles ont<br>they (feminine) have |

# Test - Niveau 1 ★ 2

Nom _____

Circle the description that matches each animal.
Be sure to pay attention to the ARTICLE!

 1) Le cobaye
La cobaye

 8) Le hamster
La hamster

 2) Les oiseaux
L'oiseau

 9) Les escargots
L'escargot

 3) Les poissons
Le poisson

 10) Le lapin
Le lapins

 4) Le dinosaure
Les dinosaures

 11) Les chiens
Le chien

 5) La grenouille
El rano

 12) Le lézard
Les lézards

 6) Le papillon
La papillon

 13) La furet
Le furet

 7) Les tortues
La tortue

 14) La chat
Le chat

# Test - Niveau 1★2

_____
Nom

> Translate each sentence into French using the verb AVOIR.

1) I have three yellow frogs.
_____

2) We have two grey cats.
_____

3) You have a white rabbit.
_____

4) He has four purple turtles.
_____

5) She has an orange bird.
_____

6) They have ten green fish.
_____

Bien fait!

That means "Well done!"

**TEACHER'S CORNER**

**Progress Score:**

Animals_____
Articles_____
Pronouns_____
"To Have"_____

QUIZ_____

Ready for Level 1-3 ? ☐

# Les Légumes

Practice writing the French word for each vegetable at least four times.

**l'artichaut**
☐ artichoke

**le poivron**
☐ bell pepper

**le brocoli**
☐ broccoli

**le chou**
☐ cabbage

# Les Légumes

le chou-fleur
☐ cauliflower

*le chou-fleur*

la carotte
☐ carrot

*la carotte*

le céleri
☐ celery

*le céleri*

le piment
☐ chili

*le piment*

# Les Légumes

le maïs
☐ corn

le concombre
☐ cucumber

l'aubergine
☐ eggplant

les haricots verts
☐ green beans

# Les Légumes

la laitue
☐ lettuce

le champignon
☐ mushroom

l'oignon
☐ onion

le petit pois
☐ pea

# Les Légumes

la pomme
de terre
☐ potato

la pomme
de terre

la citrouille
☐ pumpkin

la citrouille

la courgette
☐ zucchini

la courgette

la tomate
☐ tomato

la tomate

# Je préfère!

## QUELLE EST TA LÉGUME PRÉFÉRÉE?

Draw your favorite one of our new vegetables in the box below.

Ma légume préférée est _____.

## UNE SALADE MIXTE

Draw a picture of your favorite salad, and list at least 4 ingredients.

Ma salade a _____
_____.

# Pratique!
# VOCABULARY PRACTICE!

In the corresponding space, write the French word for each veggie.

1) _____
2) _____
3) _____
4) _____
5) _____
6) _____
7) _____

1) _____
2) _____
3) _____
4) _____
5) _____
6) _____
7) _____

# Dessine!

Draw what is described in each of the boxes below.

| | | |
|---|---|---|
| 5 carottes oranges | 2 concombres verts | Un piment rouge |
| 4 courgettes | Une aubergine | Des haricots verts |
| 2 champignons gris | Un chou-fleur blanc | 3 pommes de terre rouges |
| 2 oignons violets | 4 piments verts | Un céleri vert |

# Mots-Cachés

```
C H O U J A E D H C X W S P H
E J I P A D E X A Z E Y D E B
L S R X U E Z E R J L N C T C
E T E C B W C M I C U O H I H
R E I L E E A F C O N E O T A
I C R E R E R E O N P I U S M
N O O I G N O N T X O E F P P
H N I Y I R T E S K I E L O I
V C I N N T T H V E V K E I G
P O M M E D E T E R R E U S N
I M R E J W X O R W O L R E O
M B S E T H V M T E N S G K N
E R J L I O P A S G H K L W S
N E F T E C I T R O U I L L E Z
T O F E U S A E T P W U I L Z
```

## Banque de mots

Find the following words in French in the puzzle above.

CABBAGE    GREEN BEANS    EGGPLANT
CARROT    MUSHROOM    POTATO
CUCUMBER    CHILI    TOMATO
CELERY    ONION    BELL PEPPER
CAULIFLOWER    PUMPKIN    PEA

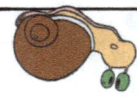

# Traductions

Translate each phrase from French to English or English to French.

1) Des aubergines roses.
_____

2) Le céleri jaune.
_____

3) La carotte bleue.
_____

4) Les céleris noirs.
_____

5) Les courgettes vertes.
_____

6) The brown mushroom.
_____

7) The orange pumpkin.
_____

8) Some black peas.
_____

9) The green beans.
_____

10) The sky blue potato.
_____

Qu'est-ce qui se cache sur cette page? What is hiding on this page?

# «Vouloir»

## The verb VOULOIR means to WANT in French.

In French, just like in English, we need to <u>conjugate</u> our verb. What that means is that we have to change it slightly so that it <u>matches</u> the person who is speaking. Then we just add the thing we want.

### Vouloir

| | | | |
|---|---|---|---|
| ☐ | je veux<br>I want | ☐ | nous voulons<br>we want |
| ☐ | tu veux<br>you want | ☐ | vous voulez<br>you (plural) want |
| ☐ | il veut<br>he wants | ☐ | ils veulent<br>they want (masc.) |
| ☐ | elle veut<br>she wants | ☐ | elles veulent<br>they want (fem.) |

### Check it out:
I want a dog.
(Je veux = I want) + (un chien = a dog).
Je veux un chien.

### Essaie!
Draw a line to match each English sentence with its French equivalent.

| | |
|---|---|
| She wants a red bell pepper. | Il veut deux oignons bleus. |
| He wants two blue onions. | Je veux cinq citrouilles oranges. |
| They want six purple artichokes. | Elle veut un pimiento rouge. |
| I want five orange pumpkins. | Ils veulent six artichauts violets. |

# Plus de traductions

Translate each phrase from French to English or English to French.

1) Je veux quatre citrouilles et un concombre.
___

2) Nous voulons un céleri et des carottes.
___

3) Elle ne veut pas de champignons.
___

4) Ils ont une tomate mais (but) veulent du chou-fleur.
___

5) Le chien ne veut pas de laitue.
___

6) You want cabbage.
___

7) We want six green tomatoes.
___

8) She doesn't want your broccoli.
___

9) They want three yellow onions.
___

10) He wants a purple eggplant but he has a green zucchini.
___

Qu'est-ce qui se cache sur cette page? What is hiding on this page?

# Lis!

Read the paragraph, then answer the questions below.

Je m'appelle Lulu, ma mamam et moi allons (we go) beaucoup au supermarché. Je veux toujours (always) acheter (to buy) des légumes. Je veux des champignons, un concombre, une laitue, et des carottes. Ma maman veut une auvbergine, une courgette et un brocoli, mais mon papa ne veut pas d'aubergine. Il veut des pommes de terre, des haricots verts et un maïs. J'ai un frère (brother). Mon frère ne veut pas de haricots verts mais quiere lechuga y champignons.

1) Qu'est-ce que Maman veut au supermarché?
_____

2) Qu'est-ce que Lulu veut au supermarché?
_____

3) ¿Qu'est-ce que le papa de Lulu veut?
_____

4) Qu'est-ce que le papa de Lulu ne veut pas?
_____

5) Qu'est-ce que le frère de Lulu veut?
_____

# Description Visuelle

Read the paragraphs below.
Draw what it says inside the box.

Bob a une grande salade avec beaucoup de laitue, deux carottes, quatre concombres, et trois tomates. Il veut cinq pommes de terre violettes.

Bob

Rébé a faim et elle veut de la soupe avec huit pois, un céleri, un oignon, sept champignons, trois aubergines et neuf haricots verts....oh! elle a très (very) faim et elle veut aussi (also) de la citrouille dans sa soupe.

Rébé

# La Révision

## Les Légumes:

## Pronoms y Vouloir:

| Je veux<br>I have | nous voulons<br>we have |
|---|---|
| tu veux<br>you have | vous voulez<br>you (plural) have |
| Il veut<br>he has | ils veulent<br>they (masculine) have |
| Elle veut<br>she has | elles veulent<br>they (feminine) have |

# Test - Niveau 1 ★ 3

Nom _____

Draw a line to match each vegetable with its name in French!

1)  le poivron    le chou    l'artichaut

    le céleri    la laitue    l'oignon

2)  la carotte    le chou-fleur    le brocoli

    le concombre    la tomate    l'aubergine

3)  le champignon    la courgette    le petit pois

    les haricots verts    la pomme de terre    le piment

Fill in the blanks to write the name of each vegetable in French!

4)  __ __ t __ e __

5)  __ __ a __

# Test - Niveau 1 ★ 3  _____
Nom

> Translate each sentence into French using the verb VOULOIR.

1) I want three purple carrots.
   _____

2) We want two yellow onions.
   _____

3) You want broccoli.
   _____

4) He wants ten red chilis!
   _____

5) She wants an orange pumpkin.
   _____

6) They want celery.
   _____

Bien fait!

That means "Well done!"

**TEACHER'S CORNER**

Progress Score:

Vegetables_____
"To Want"_____

QUIZ_____

Ready for final work ?

# Tous Ensemble

Translate each phrase from French to English or English to French.

1) J'ai dix citrouilles oranges.
   _____

2) Il veut trois papillons blancs et rouges.
   _____

3) Elles ont cinq lapins violets.
   _____

4) Nous voulons un dinosaure jaune.
   _____

5) Tu as neuf poissons roses.
   _____

6) I want seven sky blue hearts.
   _____

7) She has eight green octagons.
   _____

8) They want two brown turtles.
   _____

9) We have thirty white onions.
   _____

10) You want a grey dog.
    _____

# La Révision

Fill in the blanks to complete this review of LEVEL 1 French.

## Les nombres:

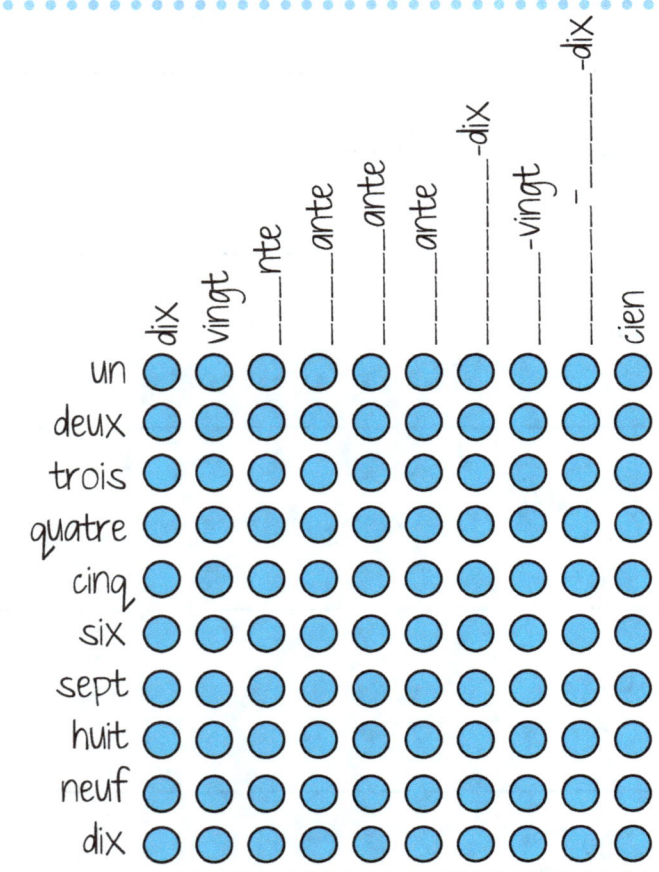

## Les formes:

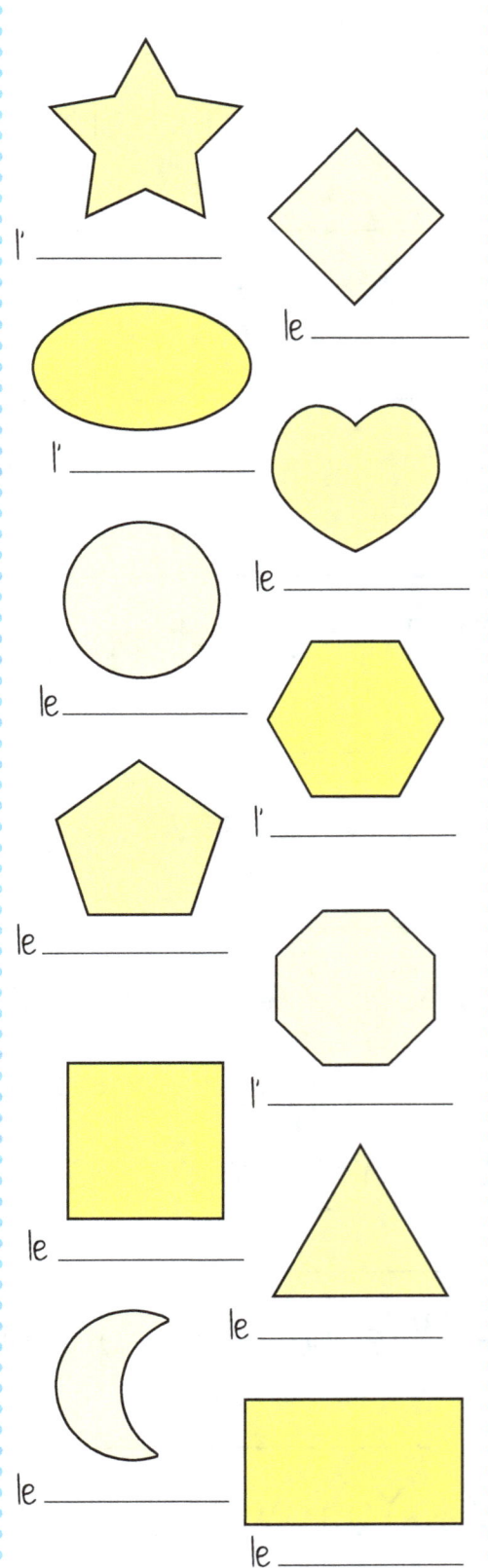

- l' _____
- le _____
- l' _____
- le _____
- le _____
- l' _____
- le _____
- l' _____
- le _____
- le _____
- le _____
- le _____

## Les couleurs:

- ros_
- ro_ge
- _range
- ja_ne
- ve_t
- bl_u
- bleu _iel
- v_olet
- mar_on

# La Révision

Fill in the blanks to complete this review of LEVEL 1 French.

## Les Animaux:

le _____   l'_____   le _____   le _____   la _____

le _____   la _____   le _____   l'_____   le _____

le _____   le _____   le _____   le _____

## Pronoms et Avoir:

| | |
|---|---|
| __'ai<br>I have | _____ avons<br>we have |
| __ as<br>you have | _____ avez<br>you (plural) have |
| __ a<br>he has | ____ ont<br>they (masculine) have |

# La Révision

Fill in the blanks to complete this review of LEVEL 1 French.

## Les Légumes:

## Pronoms et Vouloir:

| | |
|---|---|
| je veu_<br>I have | nous voul___<br>we have |
| tu veu_<br>you have | vous voul__<br>you (plural) have |
| il veu_<br>he has | ils veul___<br>they (masculine) have |

# Test Final - Niveau 1

Nom _____

Draw a line to match each picture with its correct description. Note that you will not use all of the phrases. Pay special attention to article and gender.

| | | | |
|---|---|---|---|
| ⭐ | le croissant blanc<br><br>l'étoile orange | ◆ | le losange noir<br><br>le coeur jaune |
| 🟢 (ovale) | l'étoile jaune<br><br>l'ovale vert | 💜 (coeur) | l'hexagone gris<br><br>l'octogone rouge |
| 🔴 (cercle rose) | le carré jaune<br><br>l'ovale vert | ⬢ (gris) | le losange noir<br><br>le coeur violet |
| ⬠ (pentagone) | le cercle rose<br><br>le cercle bleu ciel | 🟧 (octogone) | l'hexagone rouge<br><br>l'octogone rouge |
| 🟨 (carré) | le pentagone bleu<br><br>le carré blanc | 🔺 (triangle bleu) | le triangle bleu ciel<br><br>le rectangle marron |
|  | le croissant blanc<br><br>le pentagone bleu |  | le triangle vert<br><br>le rectangle marron |

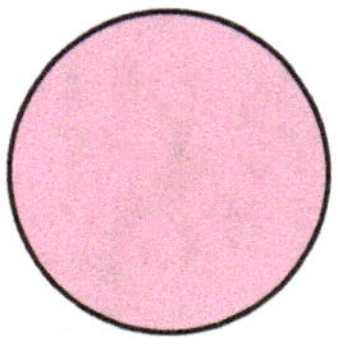

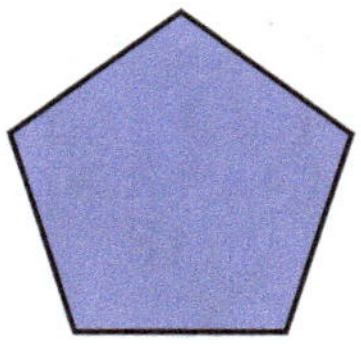

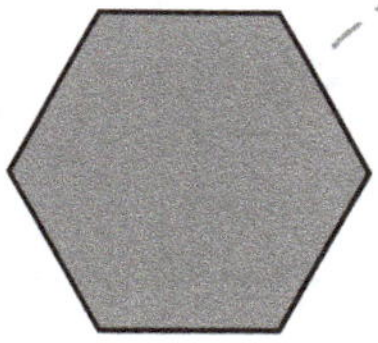

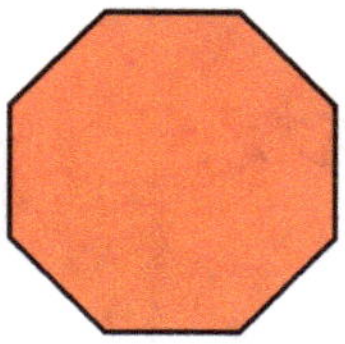

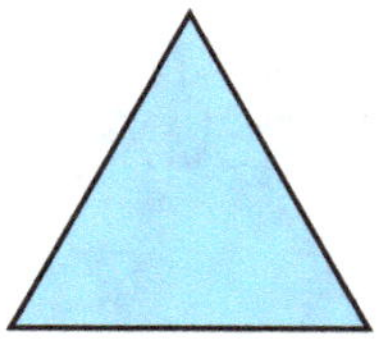

# Test Final - Niveau 1 _____
Nom

> Translate each sentence into French using the verb AVOIR.

1) I have carrots and artichokes.
   _____

2) We have lettuce and forty onions.
   _____

3) You all have broccoli.
   _____

4) He doesn't have potatoes.
   _____

5) They don't have peas.
   _____

> Read each sentence, then circle the item(s) each character has.

6) Bob a une courgette.

7) Marta a un cobaye.

8) Lily et Emma ont deux escargots.

9) Pépé a un chou-fleur et un céleri.

10) Lulú a des haricots verts et des champignons.

# Test Final - Niveau 1 _____

Nom

> Translate each sentence into French using the verb VOULOIR.

1) I want two brown dogs.
   _____

2) We want four yellow butterflies.
   _____

3) You want eight green frogs.
   _____

4) She wants fifty grey ferrets!
   _____

5) They want a blue lizard.
   _____

★★★★★★★★★★★★★ La fin ★ The end ★★★★★★★★★★★★★★

Allons-y!

That means "Let's go!"

**TEACHER'S CORNER**

Progress Score:

Level 1-1_____
Level 1-2_____
Level 1-3_____

FINAL QUIZ_____

Ready for Level 2 ?

## ¡Félicitations!

# Congratulations!

You have completed
## Level One French!

We are so very proud of you! We hope that you will use all that you have learned out in the world every day and share your love of French with everyone!

Next up?!
## Level Two French!

!À bientôt!

# français ②

Check us out on the web at
www.languagesprout.com

# Félicitations!
## Congratulations!

Nom: _____
You have completed

## Français 1

We are so proud of you!

Nous sommes très fiers de toi!

# ★ BONUS ★
## Matching Cards

Cut out the cards on the following pages and use them often!

Paste your storage envelope here.

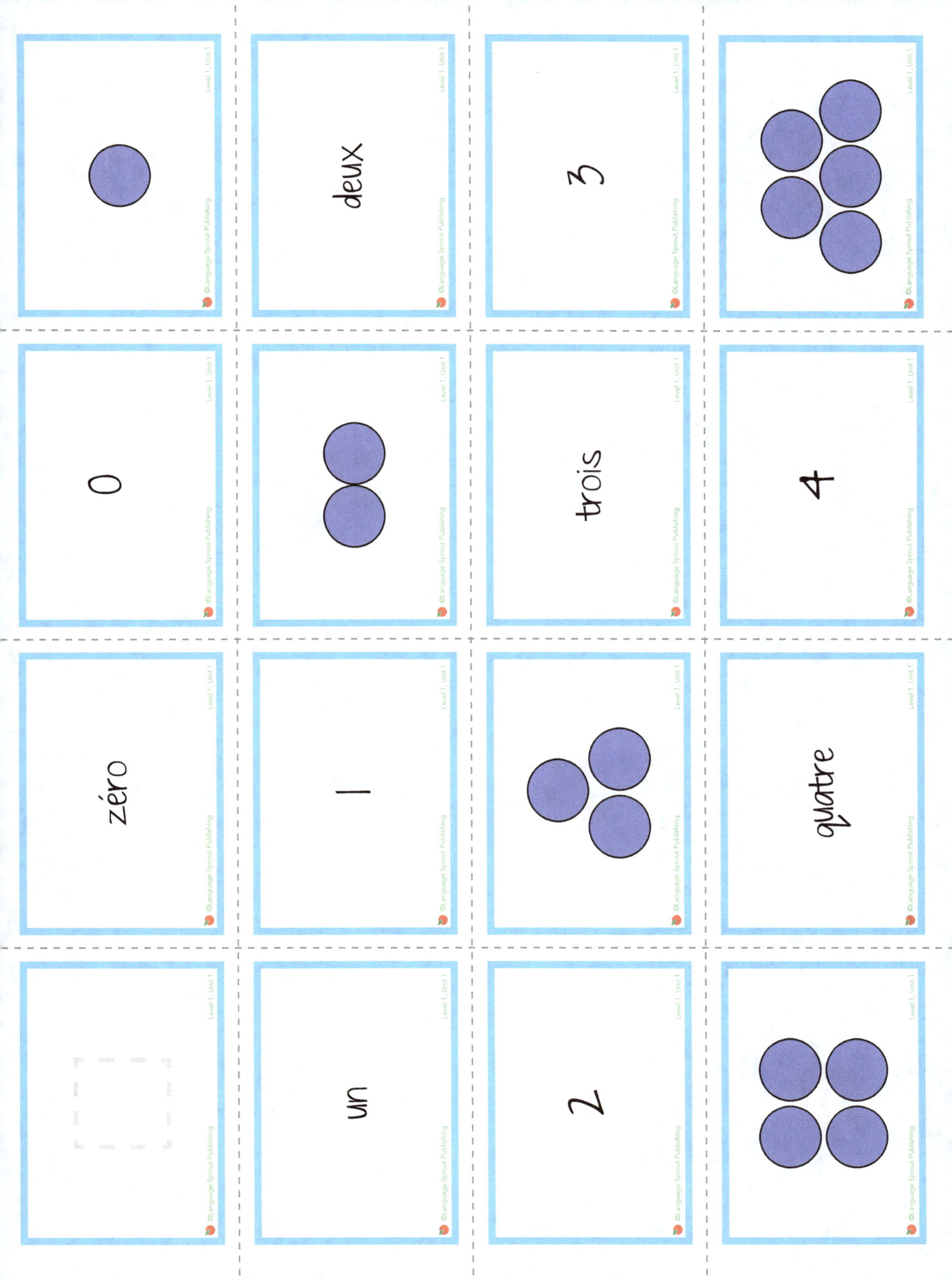

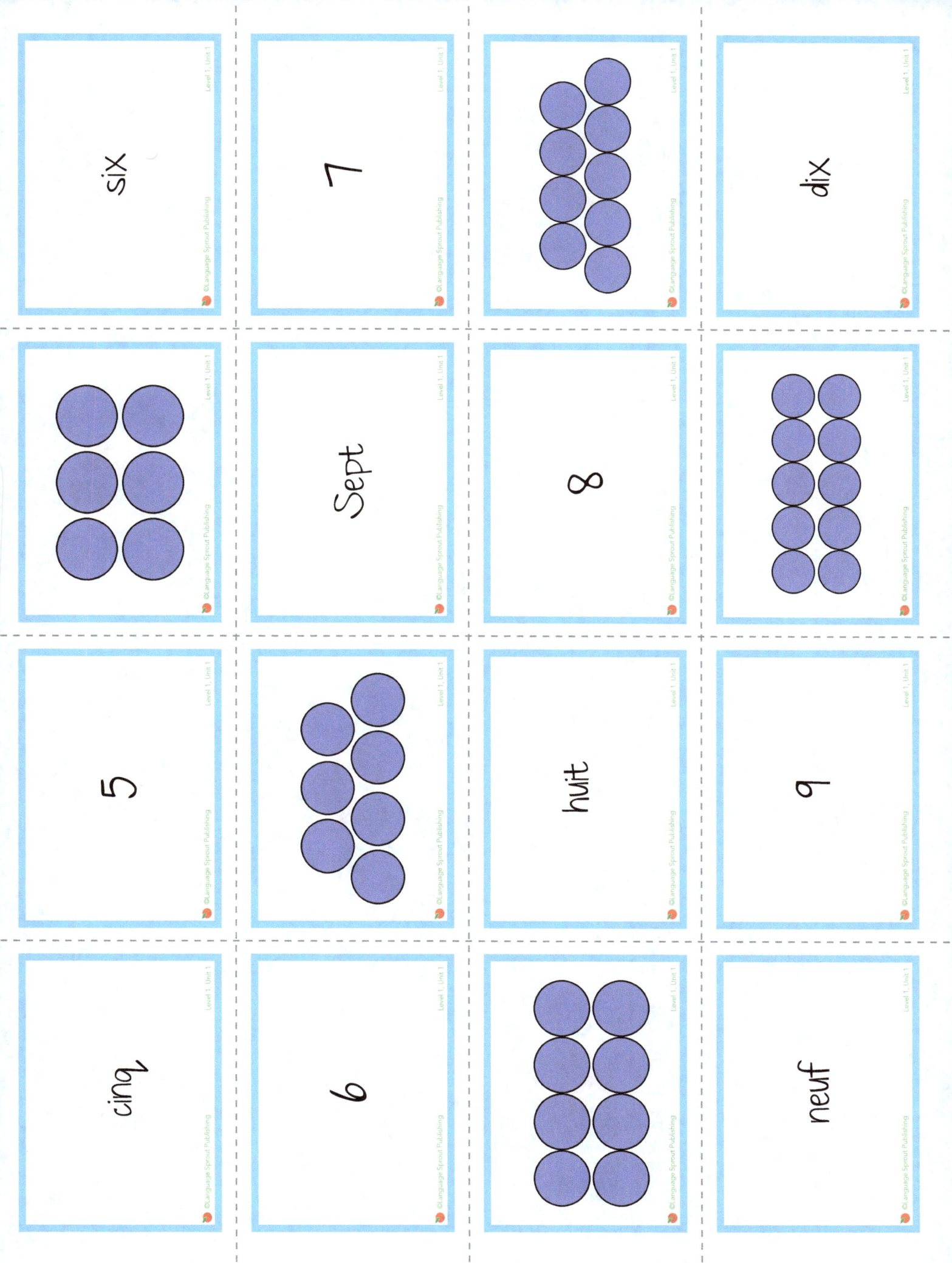

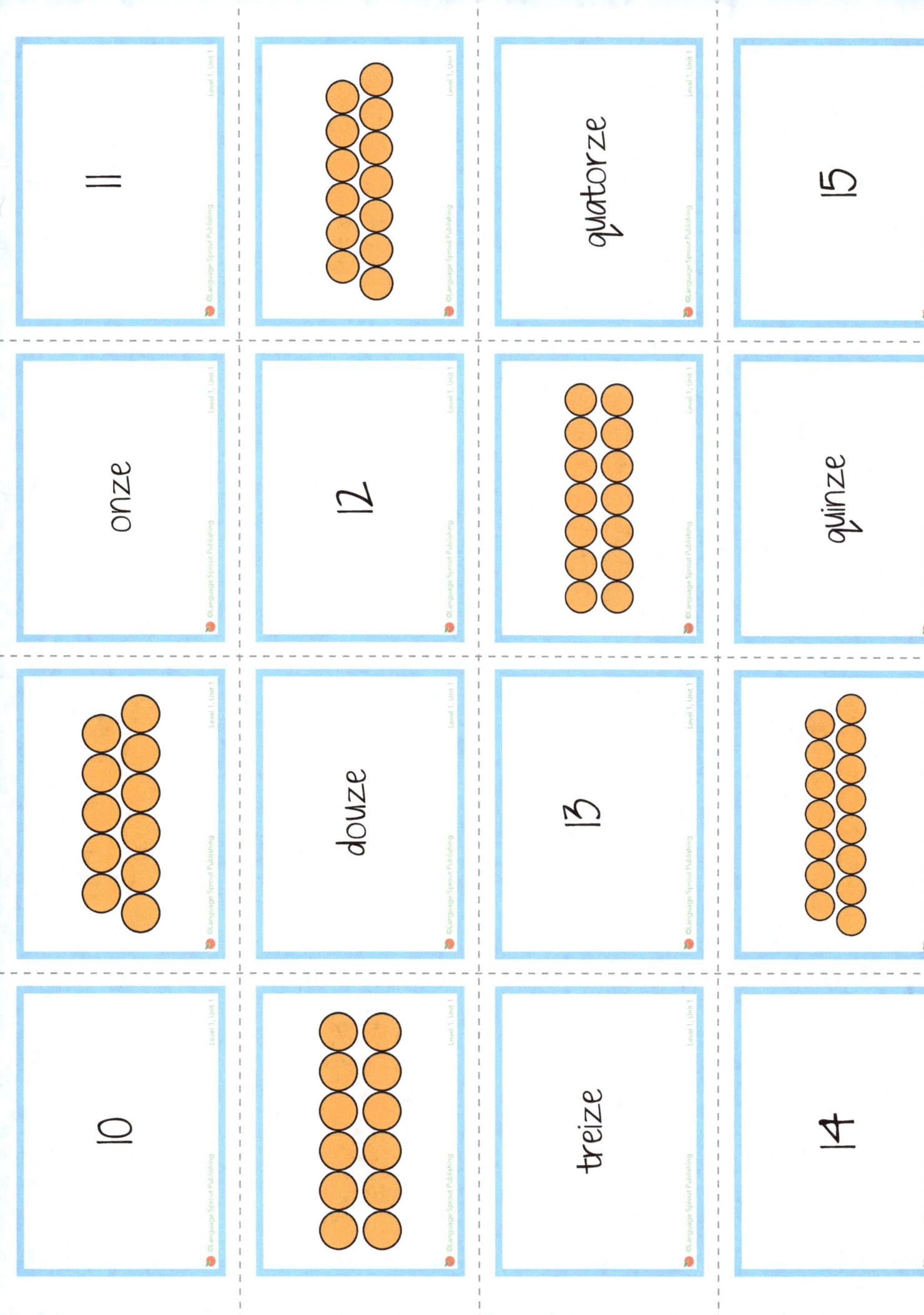

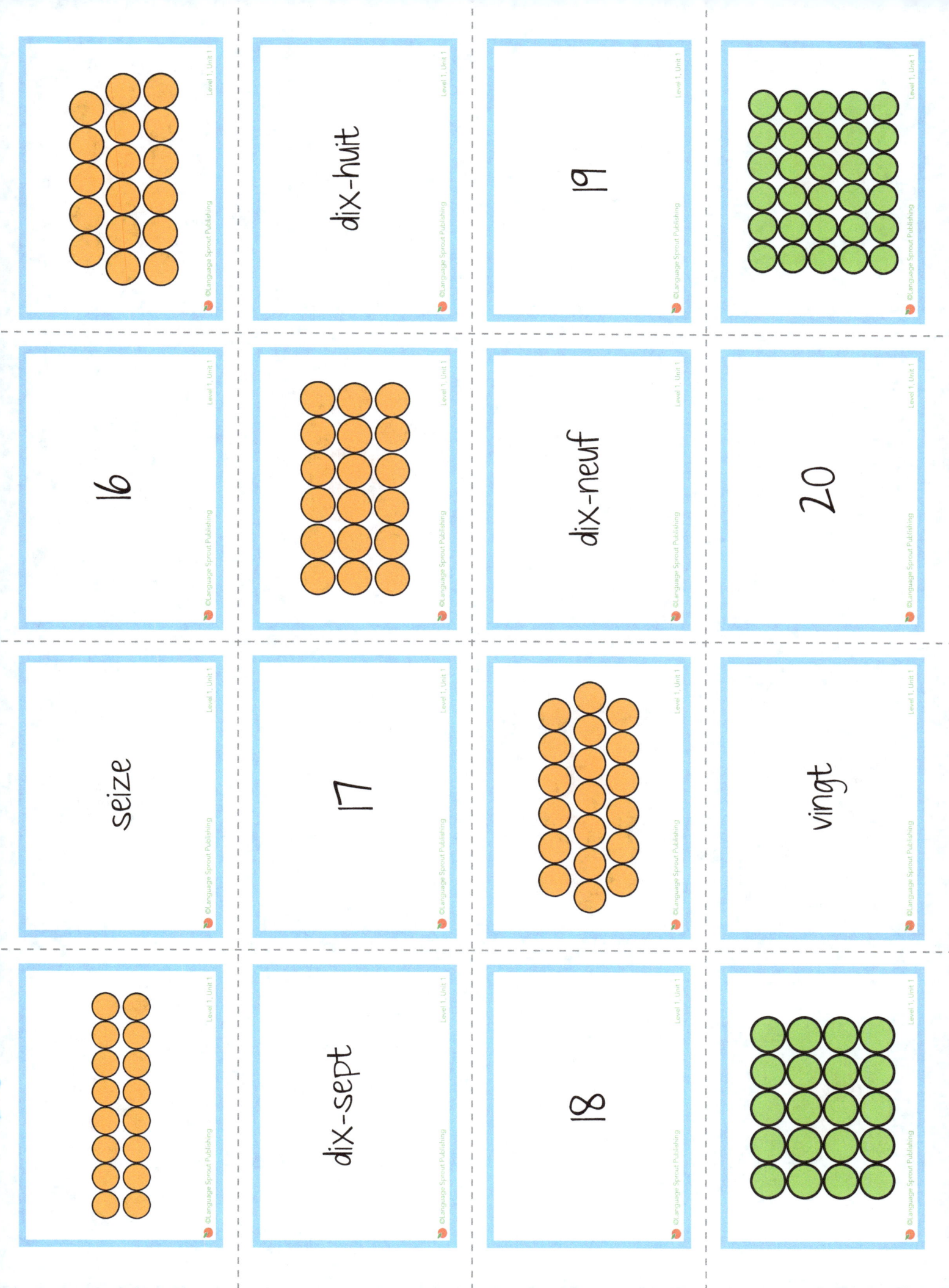

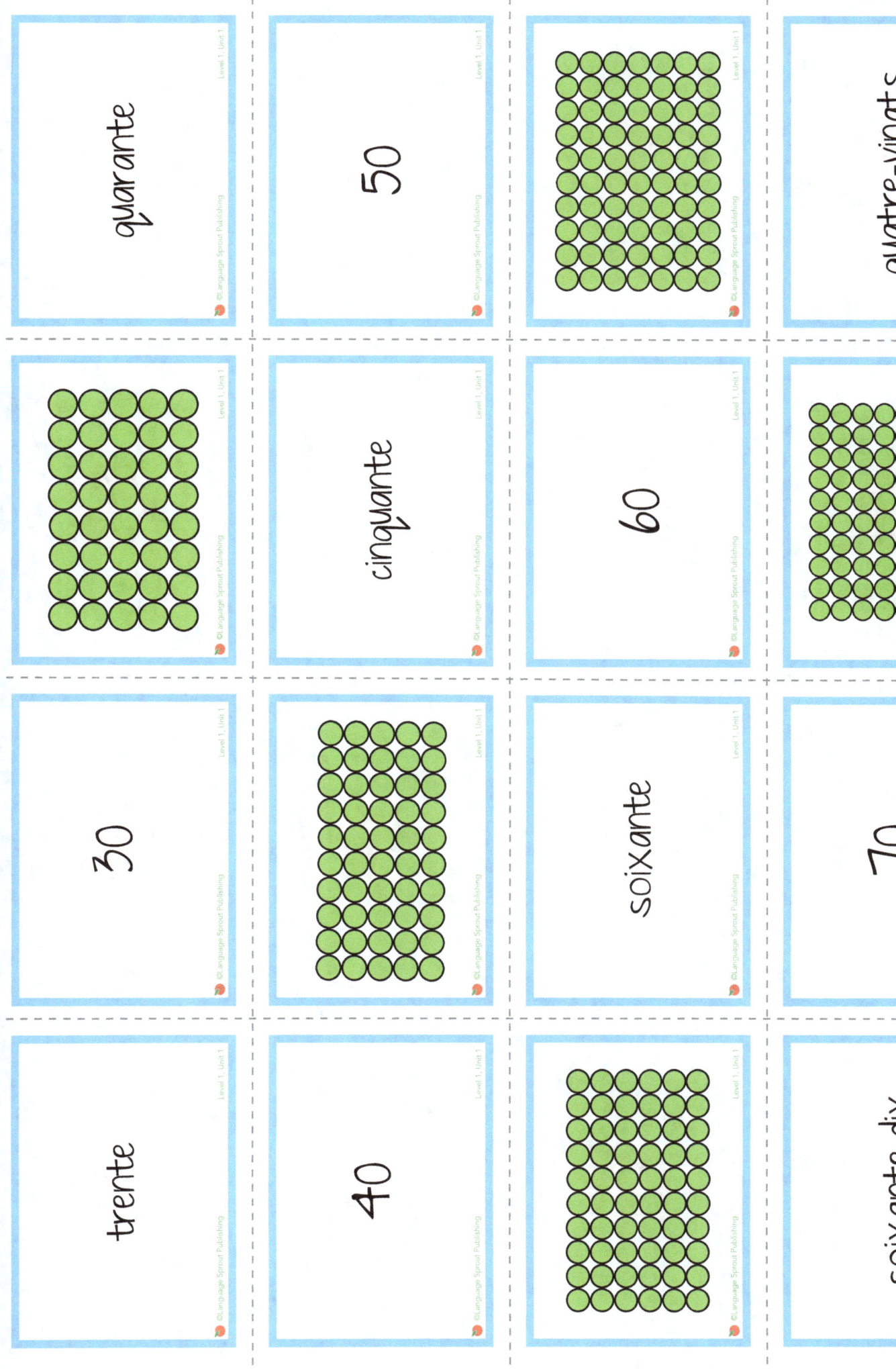

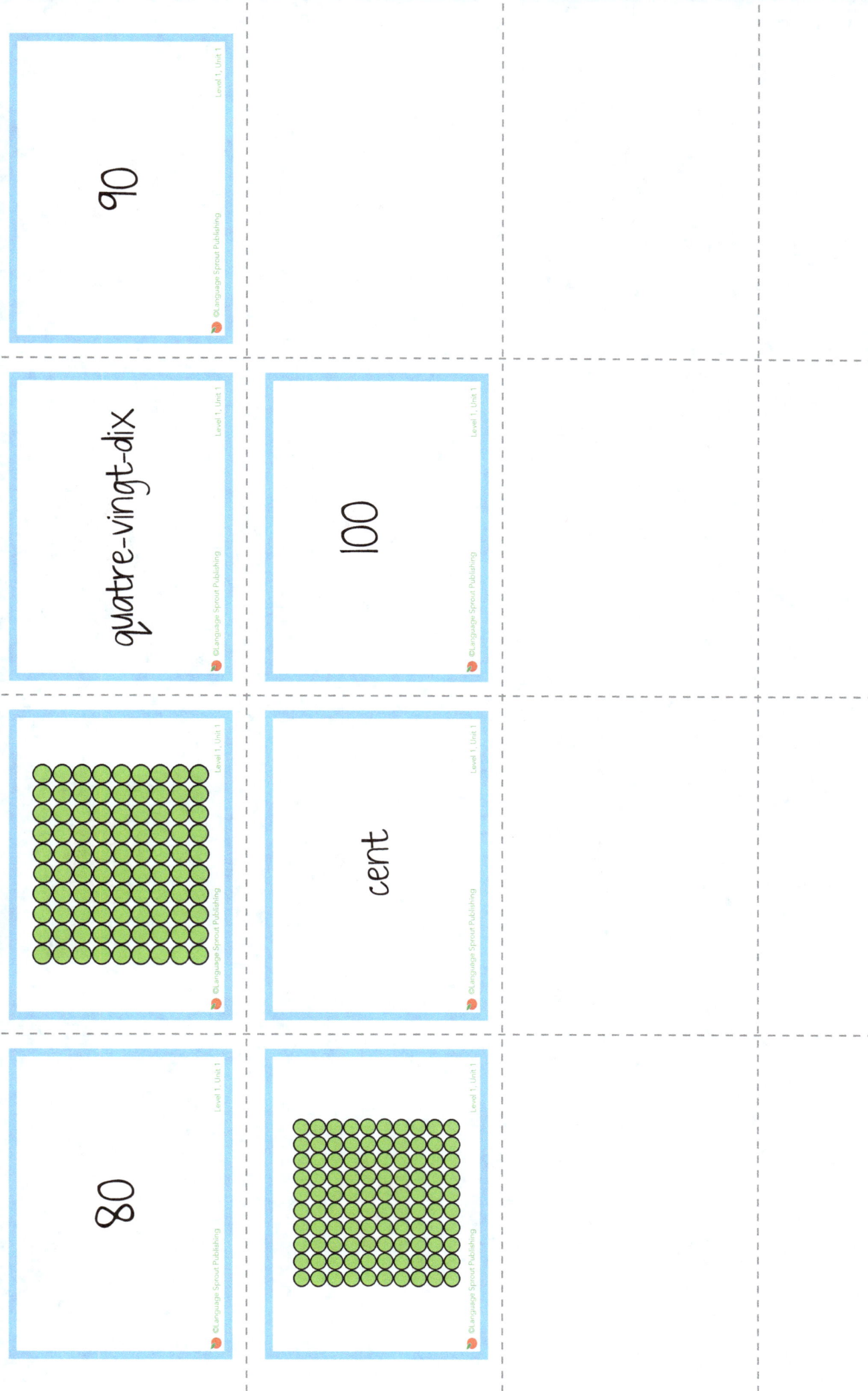

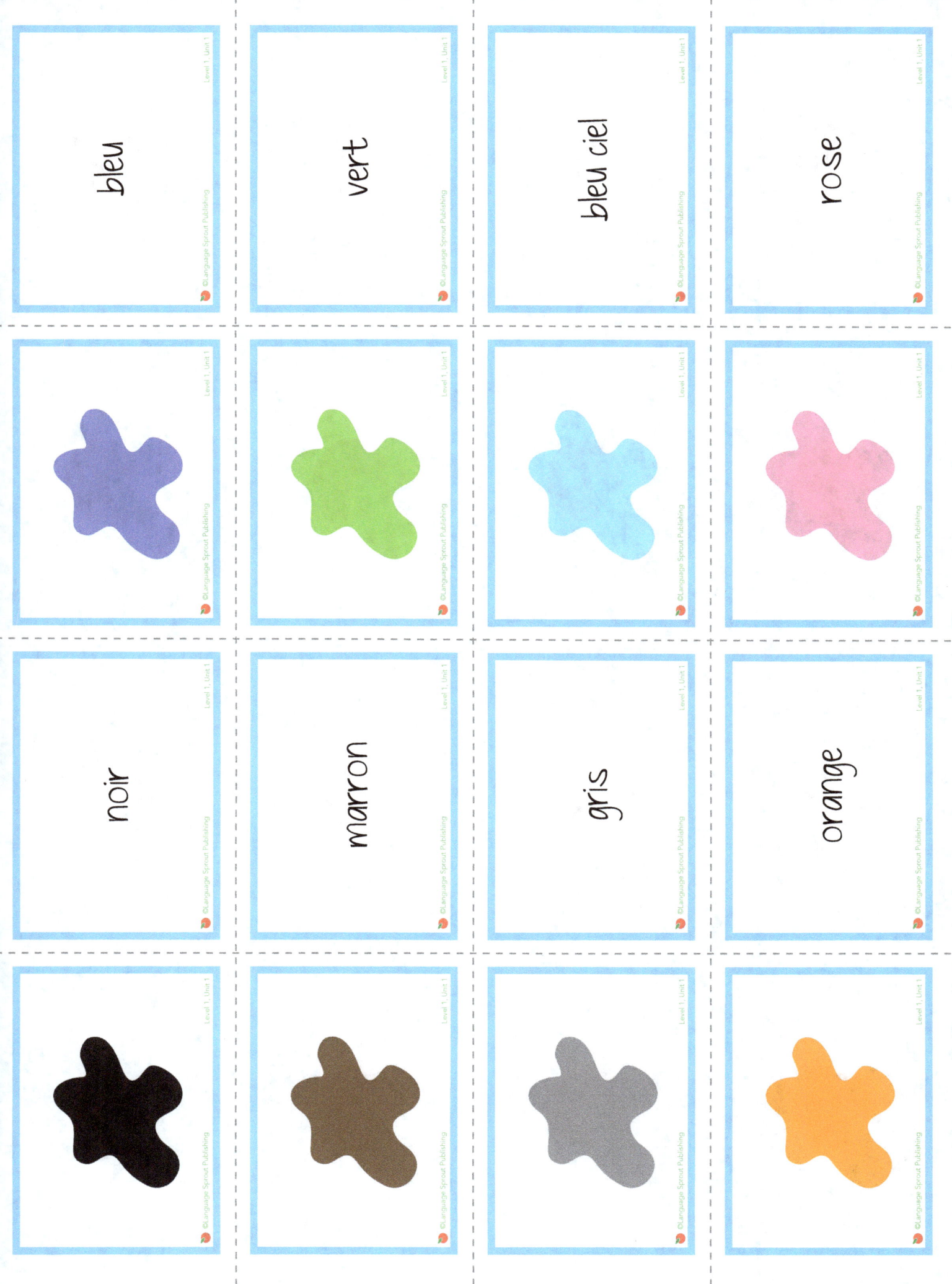

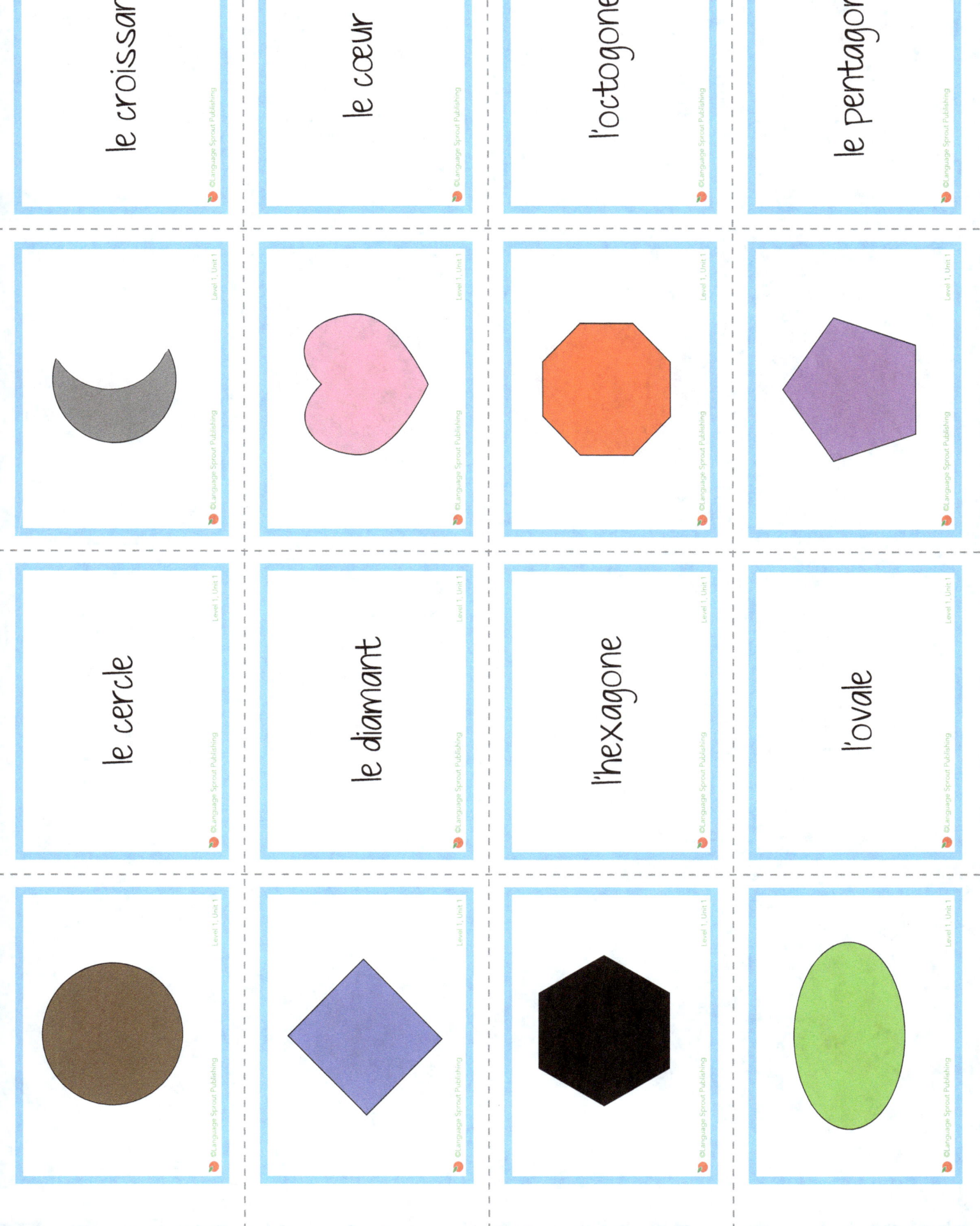

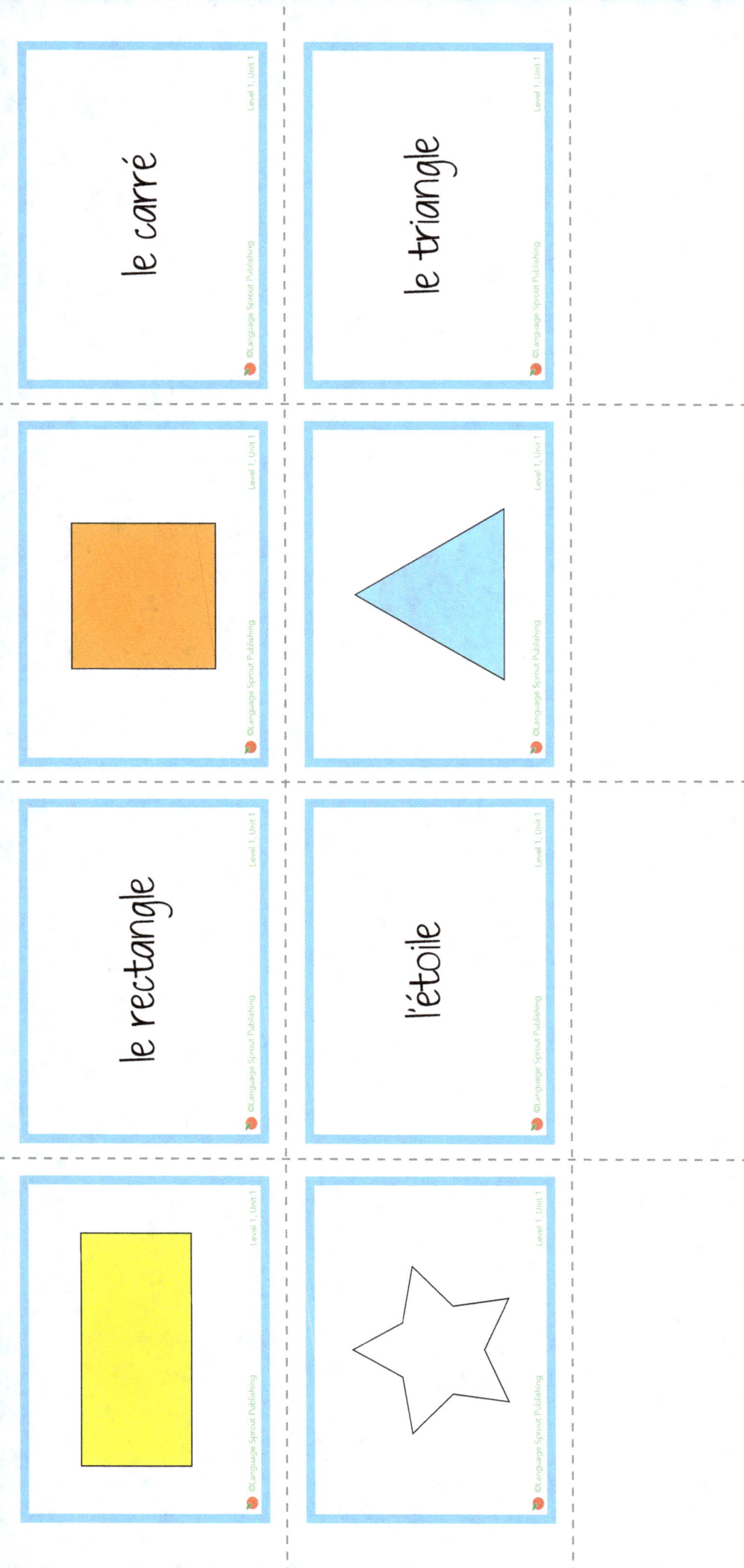

| le chat | la tortue | le cochon d'Inde | le papillon |
|---|---|---|---|
|  |  |  |  |
| le chien | l'oiseau | la grenouille | le hamster |
|  |  |  |  |

| le poivron | le chou | le chou-fleur | le piment |
|---|---|---|---|
|  | |  |  |
| l'artichaut | le brocoli | la carotte | le céleri |
|  | |  | |

| le concombre | les haricots verts | le champignon | les petits pois |
|---|---|---|---|
|  |  |  |  |
| le maïs | l'aubergine | la laitue | l'oignon |
|  | |  | |

| la citrouille | la courgette |
|---|---|
| 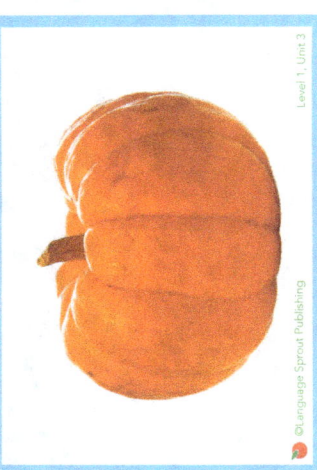 |  |
| la pomme de terre | la tomate |
|  |  |